IMAGES
of America

CHESHIRE

This book is dedicated to all of the Cheshirites who made the past I have chronicled and to the Cheshirians of the new millennium, with the admonition to remember your past, record your present, and reveal your future. I also dedicate this book to the people who have supported me in this and many other endeavors: my wife, Diane; my children, Gina and Jeff; my parents, Tony and Teresa; my brother, Jim; my mother-in-law, Doris Durand; my hometown editors, Mary Hobler Hyson and John White; and to you, who invited this book to live in your library.

IMAGES
of America

CHESHIRE

Ron Gagliardi

ARCADIA
PUBLISHING

Published by Arcadia Publishing
Charleston, South Carolina

Library of Congress Catalog Card Number: 2001089153

For all general information contact Arcadia Publishing at:
Telephone 843-853-2070
Fax 843-853-0044
E-mail sales@arcadiapublishing.com
For customer service and orders:
Toll-Free 1-888-313-2665

Visit us on the Internet at www.arcadiapublishing.com

Don Hofer is the artist who adorned a plain brick wall with this "timely" mural that has been enjoyed by so many visitors to the Watch Factory Shoppes. He was commissioned by the late Daniel Ulbrich, developer, whose vision gave new life to the factory, former Seabury Hall dormitory for Cheshire Academy, by transforming it into a commercial shopping center.

CONTENTS

ACKNOWLEDGMENTS

I thank everyone who assisted me in the birth of "baby Cheshire." Special thanks go to the main advisers for this book, Clayton Crabtree and Edgar Johnson of the Cheshire Historical Society, Ed Conklin and his sisters Estelle and Elaine for scanning and copying assistance, Fred Chesson for suggesting the project, and Pam O'Neil for shepherding this book. A few people opened up their collections of Cheshire photographs and memorabilia to me. They are *Cheshire Herald* publishers Maureen and Joe Jakubisyn; *Waterbury Republican-American* owner William J. Pape II and archivist Carol Ann Brown; Ralph Edson and Judge Ray Voelker, Cheshire residents and avid collectors of the town's historical memorabilia; and Martha Lape, archivist of the First Congregational Church of Cheshire. Special thanks are owed to Amy Sutton, publisher for Arcadia, without whose kindness, understanding, and direction this book might never have been born. (Additional acknowledgments appear at the end of the book.)

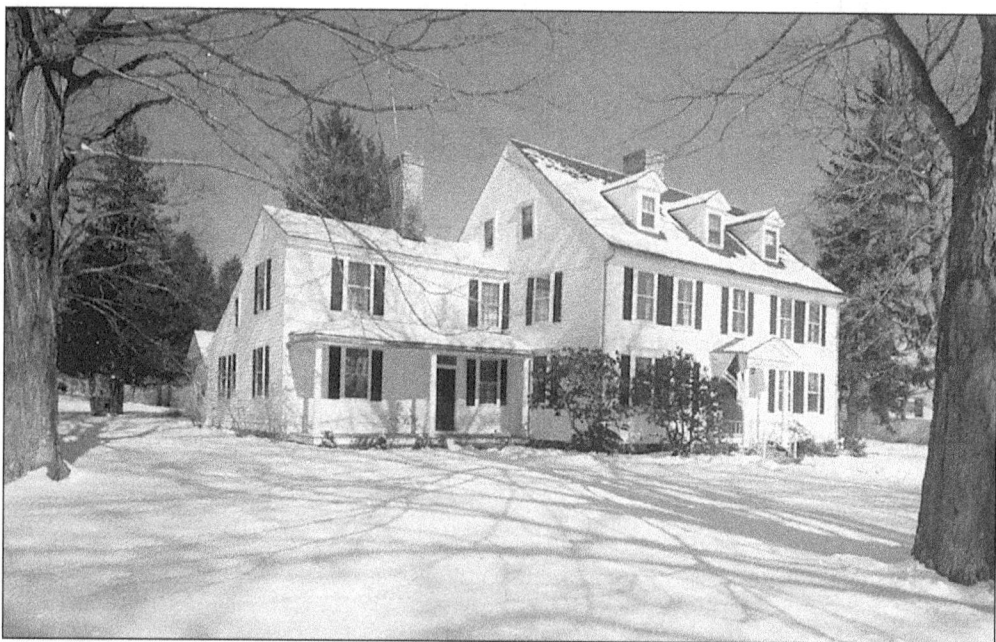

The Hitchcock-Phillips House is the hotbed of history in Cheshire. It is the home of the Cheshire Historical Society. It is a federal-style house built in 1785 for merchant Rufus Hitchcock. At one time it was owned by Cheshire Academy and was used as a dormitory. It was purchased by the town of Cheshire in 1972 and has housed the extensive holdings of the society since then.

INTRODUCTION

"You are Invited. . . ."

Welcome to Cheshire, Connecticut, my hometown. Come on in and join the history party.

This book has an interesting history of its own. I was working on a perpetual project I call the "Millennium Compendium" that is an album of Cheshire's history. An article about it appeared in local media, and Fred Chesson, a reader of the *Waterbury Republican-American*, saw it and called me to say he had some photographs and information relating to Cheshire's past. We eventually met and I learned that he is an author for Arcadia Publishing. At the time he was finishing up a book on Woodbury and had already completed books on Waterbury and New Haven.

In December 2000, Fred Chesson e-mailed me and offered to contact Arcadia Publishing on my behalf to propose a Cheshire book. Pam O'Neil sent out the proposal form, I completed it, and was accepted. I gave myself an impossible deadline and despite the urgings of my prescient wife to extend it, I finally finished the book in July 2001.

There are two morals to my story. First, do not hesitate to contact media about your projects and events; a tiny snowball of an article may unleash an avalanche of life-altering activities. Second, always listen to your wife or significant other.

One of the events that helped our town to usher in the new millennium was a contest to compose a song extolling the virtues of Cheshire. I entered (with the musical assistance of Sandra Field) but my song was not chosen. I share the lyrics with you with the hope that you will look with favor upon them and use them as an introduction to the images that follow in this book.

"It's Cheshire, Connecticut . . . My Hometown"

Where's that fine New England town where families love to live?
With proud parades and marching bands, events with thrills to give.
Celebrations, festivals and fireworks abound
In Cheshire, Connecticut . . . my hometown!

Ol' Lock 12 and Mixville Park, where people like to visit.
Linear Park, Cartoon Museum, still some folks ask, "Where is it?"
Off Eighty-Four & Six-Nine-One on Route Ten can be found
It's Cheshire, Connecticut . . . my hometown!

History and Heritage and lots of Civic Pride
Patriotism, Culture and Spirit we won't hide.
For schools and scholars, arts and sports we are most renowned.
Rams and Cats and Spartans, too, call Cheshire their hometown!

Take a walk around the Green, along our tree-lined streets
Past fine homes to the library for literary treats.
Stained-glass views and spires, too, mark well our hallowed ground
Gracing Cheshire, Connecticut . . . our hometown!

From Gateway Park, by monuments, to the Falls of Roaring Brook
On bedding farms, in orchard shade, through open-spaces nooks
We praise the name that comes with fame like jewels upon a crown
That's Cheshire, Connecticut . . . THE BEST HOMETOWN!!

CHESHIRE, CONNECTICUT . . . THE BEST HOMETOWN!!

—Copyright © 1999 by Ron Gagliardi

One

PREHISTORY

"Location. Location. Location" is the mantra of Cheshire's numerous, consistently busy real estate agents. The town is centrally located at the crossroads of Routes 10, 84, and 691. If you glance left or right as you travel on Route 691, you will see the alternating layers of arkosic sandstone, red shale, and red mudstone that was laid down at the beginning of the age of dinosaurs. This was the late Triassic period, a few hundred million years ago. Recently, the fossilized remains of an ancient reptile were found on the side of Route 691.

Then, during Steven Spielberg's favorite period, the Jurassic, the rocks were faulted and tilted toward the east. Great basaltic lava flows formed the nearby Hanging Hills and the other traprock ridges in the area.

Nothing much happened for the next 180 million years or so until the ice ages started. At least 18 times the invading ice sheets formed in the north and ground their way southward across New England, removing a little more of the underlying rock every time. About 10,000 years ago, when the last ice sheet melted away, it left a coating of glacial till, debris that was dragged along with the glacial ice. Included in the drift were several large boulders, called glacial erratics, chunks of the Hanging Hills, broken off and deposited southward. You will find them sprinkled around town. There is one on Coleman Road near Jinny Hill. The one pictured is on the corner of Country Club Road and Route 70.

Although Ye Fresh Meadows, now called Cheshire, was originally settled in 1694 by farm folk from Wallingford, Native Americans had been hunting and gathering in the fresh meadows and fine forests for at least 10,000 years. Quinnetukit, "Place of the Long River," the Native American name for Connecticut, was a popular place to hunt, fish, and raise a family, much like it is today. The Quinnipiac tribe inhabited this area. In the 1700s, there was a Native American encampment on a ridge near what is now Darcey School.

These earliest residents left behind remnants of their civilization. One such relic was discovered in Cheshire Park. Commonly called an arrowhead, the point depicted here is of the Laurentian tradition, part of the Archaic period that lasted for about 7,000 years in New England. Surprisingly, it is made from flint that may have come all the way from New York State, specifically from flint outcroppings in the Canandaigua area. It has been tentatively identified as a side-notched point, possibly of a type called a Normanskill or a Brewerton side notched. It may have found its way to this area when nomadic hunters passed through here and traded with the local residents. The Cheshire Historical Society has a display of numerous artifacts gathered from around town, many of which were discovered during plowing or the digging of foundations.

The Native American point pictured above is almost perfectly symmetrical, rare for such a primitive weapon. It was found by the author in Cheshire Park, near the parking lot.

Two

CIVILIZATION ARRIVES IN CHESHIRE

In 1637, Theophilus Eaton and John Davenport emigrated from England under a grant from the Earl of Warwick, who, according to English law, "owned" Connecticut. In 1638, Eaton and Davenport's group purchased land from its Native American owners and settled in an area west of the Connecticut River called Quinnypiack, now New Haven.

In 1667, the New Haven colonists set off a portion of their original tract, which stretched from Long Island Sound to Meriden, to form a new plantation. The village was named Wallingford, after the hometown of some of the planters. Wallingford was destined to become Cheshire's foundation when, in 1694, Wallingford residents Joseph Ives and John Hotchkiss built log homes and became the first of the "West farmers" to settle in Ye Fresh Meadows. Starting in 1718, West farmers began to petition the state's general assembly to be set off from Wallingford. At this time there were 45 families in the settlement. In 1723, West Farms was constituted as a distinct society by legislative grant under the name of the parish of New Cheshire. Thomas Brooks, who had arrived in 1705, suggested the name in honor of his home city of Cheshire, England. The parish remained in the town of Wallingford until 1780, when it was incorporated as the town of Cheshire.

The Belknap House, located at 87 Main Street, was built by Ebenezer Bunnell in 1740. The Bunnells arrived in the West Farms c. 1709 from Wallingford. They owned about 400 acres in what is currently the center of town. Spring Street was a lane that wound through their farm. The house has an interesting history, having been owned by a succession of families: the Abanatha, Jarvis, Hitchcock, Bronson, Tiley-Stevens, Baldwin, Lambo, Galucci, Allen, and Belknap families. Ira Bronson of Wolcott operated a blacksmith shop there from 1834 to 1842. Azuba Tiley and Sarilla Stevens bought the house in 1842. Their deed required that they share the abode "marked by a straight line through the middle of the house." In July 1911, Germano Galucci had a cobbler shop in the house. He added a large window that featured his work and the children's toys he produced.

The Bishop Abraham Jarvis House is still located at 125 Main Street and is over 200 years old. Bishop Abraham Jarvis moved to Cheshire from Middletown and had this house built c. 1799. He was one of the trustees of the new Episcopal Academy, which is where his son attended school. In 1829, the house was sold by the Jarvis heirs to Silas Hitchcock, a public servant of the first rank, who also owned the Belknap House. Hitchcock was a judge of probate, justice of the peace, town clerk, selectman, and served as a state representative for five terms. His relatives owned the house until the mid-1940s when it was leased to Cheshire Academy by the Kilijarvi family and Roy Wagner. In 1969, the Durkin family owned the home. The last family to live in the house was that of James Meehan. Meehan was proud to show visitors the hidden compartment in the basement where slaves traveling the Underground Railroad reportedly stayed. The building has been renovated for commercial use.

St. Peter's Church is an imposing edifice on the corner of Main and South Main Streets. In 1760, Joseph Moss deeded the land for a church, and the first structure was dedicated that winter. Within 10 years, it was replaced by a new building located on its present site that was only 42 feet square. Between 1840 and 1910, the church was added to three times. Redecorating and remodeling took place in the 1920s and the 1950s. A new parish house and church school were finished in 1958. The latest addition, opened in 2000, was designed by local architect Edward Saad and was dedicated by Rector Stephen A. Fales.

The interior of St. Peter's Church features a pipe organ and Gothic stained glass windows. It has a center aisle flanked on either side by classic wooden pews.

A gentleman of the landed gentry takes a quill in hand and pens a letter in the presence of his paramour. It is a silhouetted scene that could well have taken place in the parlor of one of Cheshire's wealthy families in the late 1700s. The word silhouette comes from the name of Etienne de Silhouette, controleur-general of France in 1757, a notoriously cheap man who was a cutout portraitist himself. The black-on-white cutout portraits were less expensive versions of the much more costly painted portraits, and the parsimonious public servant's name became derisively attached forevermore.

An old boot wired to a post often served as a mailbox in the early days of mail delivery. This drawing was featured on a commemorative postcard issued by the Cheshire Philatelic Society in May 1966.

Three

Exploring the 1800s

The population of Cheshire was 2,888 in 1800, at the start of what was to be a very prosperous century for the town. Progress was swift. The Farmington Canal ushered in a flood of increased manufacturing, starting in 1828. Factories were established to take advantage of the ease of transport. The mineral barite was discovered in 1835 and mining began. Work began on the Canal Line Railway in 1846, signaling an end to the canal. Cheshire Manufacturing Company (later to be known as the Ball and Socket Manufacturing Company) was organized in 1850. Numerous hotels and taverns served the townspeople, as well as visitors from surrounding cities and towns. Places such as the Munson Hotel, the Wallace House, and the Waverly Inn were established. Service clubs, including the Cheshire Grange and the Village Improvement Society, were organized. Cheshire was beginning to industrialize, but it was to be a long time before the town abandoned its predominately farm-community reputation.

Route 10 was already a major artery in 1801 for the stage connecting Hartford and New Haven. The road was built under the auspices of the Cheshire Turnpike Company as a toll road in 1801. Travelers paid to use it; someone would actually have to turn a pike, which was a long pole that blocked the road, to allow passage. This 1940 Christmas card evokes the feeling of the speeding stage making its way between the two cities.

Built in the mid-1700s by Abijah Beach, this elegant tavern was one of Cheshire's primary gathering spots for 100 years. The third story is a ballroom that over the years has served as a meeting place and a dance hall. In 1852, the building was purchased by Martin Brennan, who made it a private residence. However, Brennan allowed Catholic services in the ballroom from 1856 to 1859. Research in the possession of current owners, the Gaudios, reveals that the tavern was once called the Ben Franklin Inn and that Franklin himself performed surveying for the U.S. post office in the area.

The Governor Foote House is located at 219 South Main Street. Yale graduate Rev. John Foot had this house built c. 1767. Foot was the husband of Abigail Hall, daughter of Rev. Samuel Hall, the pastor of the First Congregational Church. For 46 years, Foot ministered to the people of Cheshire. His son Samuel Augustus Foot, born on November 8, 1780, grew up to become a congressman, a senator, and governor of Connecticut in 1834. By this time, an "e" had been added to the last name. Edith Cornell, the last individual owner of the house, sold the property in 1973 to the Connecticut Savings Bank. Today, it is the First Union Bank and a site on Cheshire's Patriot Trail because the governor's son, Adm. Andrew Hull Foote, also lived here.

This Second Empire period home with a mansard roof is now called the Amos Baldwin-Johnson House. Prominently located at 84 Main Street, across from the cemetery of St. Peter's Church, it was built in 1800 and for a time was owned by the Episcopal Academy. It has been the home of the Johnson family for four generations. The current resident is Joseph Edgar Beadle Johnson, a curator, board member, and mainstay of the Cheshire Historical Society.

Originally built in 1801 by Russell Cook, this home at 163 South Main Street has also been a tavern, a school, and the home to the first telephone exchange in Cheshire. For years, lawyers Phil Reed and Tom Jackson housed their law firm here. The house is now occupied by lawyer Robert L. Sweeney Jr.

This mantelpiece masterpiece is one of the earliest known paintings of Cheshire. It adorns a fireplace in the Cheshire Historical Society, at 43 Church Drive, by the green. It has been attributed to Sylvester Hall, a limner. These artists often crushed minerals to make their own pigments and sometimes managed to squeeze some silver or gold from patrons' purses in return for creative signs, portraits, and landscapes. The church depicted is the First Congregational Church at its second site, located near where the Civil War Monument is now. The picture was painted prior to 1827, when the church was constructed at its present location.

This saltbox-style house, originally located at 242 South Main Street, was built by Selden Spencer probably prior to 1800. Thomas Kensett bought the house in 1813. He was the father of John Frederick Kensett, the acclaimed artist of the Hudson River school of painters, who was born here in 1818. The younger Kensett attended the Episcopal Academy for a short time and helped at his father's engraving shop, which was located on Blacks Road. The house burned down and Slater Funeral Home now occupies the site. In an ironic twist of history, a memorial service to honor the 125th anniversary of his death was held on the site of his birth in 1997. The actual eulogy was reread by Joseph Trifilo. Kensett's favorite hymn, Nearer My God to Thee, was played by Sterling Jewett, and a full Masonic ceremony was conducted by Cheshire Temple Lodge No. 16.

The Farmington Canal opened in Cheshire in 1828, permitting additional trading and manufacturing opportunities for town businesses. It was open to barge traffic from 1828 to 1848. Lock 12 in Cheshire is the only lock along the entire length of the canal that has been restored. The Amistad captives passed through Cheshire and Lock 12 in 1839 on their way from New Haven to Farmington and continued on to Hartford for trial. There is also a small museum near the gatekeeper's house that is shown in the picture. The site is listed in the National Register of Historic Places.

The illustration from a commemorative envelope shows a barge leaving Lock 12 of the Farmington Canal. Artist Hans Bauer has depicted horses on the towpath and men with a chain and a pole or pike guiding the barge away from the stone walls. A street nearby the canal is called Towpath Lane. The envelope was created and sold by the Cheshire Philatelic Society to celebrate Cheshire's bicentennial in 1980.

Another commemorative envelope from Cheshire's bicentennial celebration features an etching of the First Congregational Church and the green c. 1835. The church was built in its third location during 1826 and 1827 and was designed by the well-known architect David Hoadley. Travelers headed north on what is now South Main Street were treated to this view of the green.

Munson's was originally a tavern and a store. Levi Munson one of the clerks, ended up owning the store. In 1850, Munson purchased the hotel and ran it for 30 years. His son-in-law, Franklyn Wallace, then took over, turning the hotel into a resort for visitors coming to the countryside from New Haven and the surrounding area. The entire complex was destroyed in a fire on October 28, 1892.

Loren Humiston married Howard Moss in 1854, and the couple purchased the property at 92 Main Street. They added the current house to a small building and loft that were already on the property. The Humiston and Williams families occupied the house until 1938. It was then bought by Dr. and Mrs. Robert Craig. The current owner is Joe Mayo, who conducts his advertising company at that address.

This photograph dates from c. 1860. The beautiful, Victorian-style house, located at 253 West Main Street, is currently owned by Clifton and Mary Hartman. The home has changed very little over the years. The intricate decorative work on the exterior is sometimes referred to as gingerbread.

This home, located at 466 Academy Road, was built in 1857 by Nathan Booth, a part-time farmer and civil engineer. A daughter, Sarah Booth, married Clarence Williams of Manchester and lived in the house. Their daughter, Elizabeth Williams, married Samuel L. Norton and had two children, Birdsey and Ruth Norton. In 1930, Birdsey Norton was elected selectman. He later became first selectman and served until his death, on July 25, 1954. A favorite story about him begins with a complaint from an upset woman concerning the milkman's horse leaving "road apples" in front of her house every morning. Norton reportedly said, "If only I were that regular." The Happy Time Nursery School was run at the Academy Road home for years by Ruth Norton, and the agriculture business is now operating under the name of the Norton Brothers Fruit Farm.

This photograph portrays a not-so-common sight, It is a tombstone in the front yard of a private residence near the center of town. It is the grave of the former owner, John C. Johnson, a local basket weaver who died on April 17, 1852, at the age of 75. He wanted to be buried with his pet. The pet's tombstone, now disintegrated, read simply, "A Noble Cat."

The Ives-Anderson House was constructed by Titus B. Ives in 1857. Titus B. Ives was the son of Sen. Benajah Ives, one of the founders of the Cheshire Manufacturing Company. The younger Ives became superintendent of the factory after it had become the Ball and Socket Manufacturing Company. The Ives family owned the residence until 1943, when it was purchased by Irving B. Anderson, the developer of Honey Pot Glen. The land in back of the home, located at 383 West Main Street, had seven outbuildings, including an icehouse, fruit house, and carriage house. The current owners, Eric and Laura Pagliaro Anderson, have spent countless hours and untold dollars in their continuing efforts to renovate and restore the home.

Practicing for war is not normally sandwiched between mathematics and science in the curriculum, at least not in Cheshire. However, in the 1860s, drill was required at the renamed Episcopal Academy Military School. This picture was taken c. 1868. The school itself was founded in 1794 as the Episcopal Academy and is the oldest boarding school still operating on its original site in the country. It is now called Cheshire Academy. The academy has had many distinguished graduates, staff, and administrators in its 200-plus years of existence.

These nine cadets posing for the photographer also pose a bit of a mystery. The picture is labeled on the back as a Cheshire photograph. One of the cadets has the letters CA (possibly Cheshire Academy) on his collar. Two others have CMA (possibly Cheshire Military Academy) or EMA (Episcopal Military Academy) on their collars. But Ann Moriarty, the archivist of Cheshire Academy, maintains that there never was a CMA or an EMA. However, there is a postcard labeled Cheshire Military Academy (see page 76). A cadet corps uniform from Cheshire Academy is on display at the Cheshire Historical Society.

John F. Kensett was born in Cheshire in 1818. He attended the Episcopal Academy and helped in his father's engraving shop. He apprenticed to his uncle, Alfred Daggett, who was a banknote engraver in New Haven. Kensett studied painting in England from 1840 to 1845 and traveled in Europe until 1848. He returned to the United States and became a prominent member of the Hudson River school of painting. He was one of three people named by the president to the prestigious United States Capitol Art Committee. Kensett died in 1872. His paintings now sell in the million-dollar range. His work is represented in major collections, including the Wadsworth Atheneum in Hartford, Metropolitan Museum of Art in New York (of which he was a founder and board member), New Britain Museum of American Art, and Yale University Art Gallery in New Haven. A major retrospective of his work was held recently at the Mattatuck Museum in Waterbury.

Wealthy publisher Joseph Beach (1828–1911) stands at the gate in this portrait taken between 1874 and 1878. He had retired from business in 1865 to pursue other interests, including authoring A *History of Cheshire, 1694–1840*, which was published by the Daughters of the American Revolution in Cheshire. The building still stands today, a few houses down from Cornwall Avenue, at 273 South Main Street.

From 1858 to 1889, an eccentric homeless man wandered over a 365-mile area that encompassed a circuit between the Connecticut and Hudson Rivers. His route caused him to appear at the same location every 34 days. He passed through Cheshire as well as Hamden, Meriden, and Middletown. His name was Jules Bourglay. Originally from France, Bourglay suffered a business reversal in a leather deal that cost him his marriage and, perhaps, his sanity. He emigrated to the United States, where he traveled on foot for over 30 years, clad in a rough-hewn leather coat, staying in caves and living on charity. He was found dead in a cave on the Dell farm in Mount Pleasant, New York, on Sunday, March 24, 1889. His life was chronicled on a Connecticut Public Television program entitled *The Last Circuits of the Leatherman*.

Welcome to the state-of-the-art kitchen of the 1800s. Only the latest conveniences are used here. Note the hanging cast-iron pots for breakfast porridges, lunchtime soups, and supper stews. Observe the fine, brick-lined cooking hearth. There is even a high-tech food processor and robber repellent hanging beneath the mantel. This particular kitchen is in the Hitchcock-Phillips house, once a dormitory for Cheshire Academy. It is now the home of the Cheshire Historical Society.

The mineral barite was discovered in Cheshire in 1840. An older black woman named Jinny was rumored to have found chunks of the white rock in her garden. Jinny Hill Road is supposedly named after her. However, there is an alternate explanation for the name that the author came across by chance in Webster's dictionary. The term *Jinny road* is defined as "in mining, an inclined railroad which loaded cars descend by their own weight, causing empty cars to ascend. (Brit)." It is possible that such a setup was in operation in the mine and the Cornish miners named the nearby road Jinny Hill after the British term.

Imagine a world of underground darkness, pierced only by candlelight or oil lamps. This was the daily world of the hundreds of miners, many from Cornwall, England, who were employed in the mines. Danger was a daily companion. One cave-in occurred in 1850, imprisoning James Lanyon, the superintendent, and three others. Fortunately, they were rescued. Lanyon Drive is named after Lanyon. There is an envelope addressed to him on page 38. The barite mines in Cheshire were worked until 1878. These mines produced thousands of tons of sulfate of barite, used in the production of glass, paint, cloth, and some rubber products.

This is a chunk of barite on display at the Peabody Museum in New Haven. It is also called heavy spar. A few pieces of it are displayed in the Cheshire Historical Society as well.

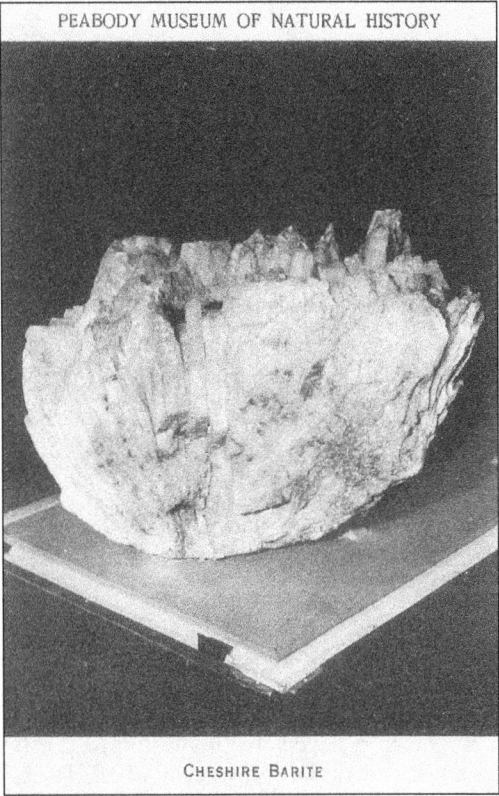

PEABODY MUSEUM OF NATURAL HISTORY

CHESHIRE BARITE

Oxen teams were used to haul the barite from the mines to the loading dock for the Farmington Canal, on Higgins Road. After the canal closed, the loads were shipped by railroad from the same location.

ANNIVERSARY SOCIABLE.

L. U.

Mr. _E B Jeralds_

The pleasure of your company, with Ladies, is
requested at the Anniversary Sociable of the L. U. Society,
at Town Hall, Cheshire, Dec. 16, 1875.

E.B. Jeralds received this invitation to the L.U. Society's Anniversary Sociable, held at the Cheshire Town Hall on December 16, 1875. The card reveals the price, the entertainment, the names of the committee, but not the time, nor what the L.U. Society was. This is another mystery for future history sleuths.

This stately Victorian house was originally built for the Jeralds family. Mr. Jeralds was a wealthy businessman whose company, Jeralds and Lawton, produced metal products, including needles. It has been renovated and has served as a popular gathering place for local residents. Called the Victorian House, but referred to as the "Vic House" by local afficionados, it has been in operation for approximately 20 years under the ownership of Tom Rose and Ed Fitzgerald.

The First Congregational Church of Cheshire has a beautiful, well-lit interior. This photograph was taken some years ago, and many changes have been made to the altar area over the intervening years.

There have been many photographs taken of the front of the First Congregational Church on the Cheshire Green. It is one of the most common images of Cheshire one encounters on postcards. This rare shot of the back of the church is dominated by a giant Japanese chestnut tree. It resembles a multitentacled octopus and is like the quintessential "spreading chestnut tree" made famous by Henry Wadsworth Longfellow in his poem *The Village Blacksmith*. The tree was planted *c.* 1876, probably by Tilton Munson or his son. Pollen from this tree was used to develop hybrid, blight-resistant trees to replace the chestnut trees that had been decimated by disease. These special chestnut trees now grow all over New England and as far south as North Carolina. Scientists from the Connecticut Agricultural Experiment Station continue to collect and utilize the pollen to this day.

St. Bridget's Church was originally located on Highland Avenue on an acre of land donated by Michael Garde in 1859. The cemetery is still there. The church in its early years is shown on this postcard.

St. Bridget's Church, Cheshire, Conn.

St. Bridget's was enlarged in 1883 and a bell tower, a marble altar, and stained glass windows were added. The church moved to Main Street in 1957, and the new building was dedicated on December 7, 1958.

The Cheshire Watch Company opened in 1883. George Capewell was the president, and E.R. Brown and D.A. Bucks were his partners. Many Cheshire watches were sold, but the company faced numerous problems with its watchmaking machinery (depicted below) and was forced to close in 1891. The building eventually became Seabury Hall for the Cheshire Academy and was transformed into the Watch Factory Shoppes in 1979.

This is an interior view of the Cheshire Watch Company, featuring the watchmaking machinery that caused the company problems.

In the late 1880s, businesses around the country were approached by specialized companies and urged to sponsor large engravings of aerial views of their town or city. Cheshire had its portrait done in 1882 by the O.H. Bailey Company of Boston. This postcard-sized version was given out "Compliments of Waverly Inn Club, Cheshire, Conn." It portrays a small community centered around a few main streets with factories and lots of land.

By 1894, Cheshire had 12 school districts with approximately 350 students. This picture of a class in West Cheshire was taken on May 2, 1887, and shows an integrated school with 38 students and 2 teachers. The photograph was donated to the Cheshire Historical Society by Mrs. William Shay and has the name Raymond W. Smith on the back.

Elegant lodging and fine dining were always available at the Wallace House on the green. This is a later version of the same building shown in the etching on page 20. Franklyn Wallace took it over from Levi Munson in 1880, and operated it as a resort until it was consumed by fire in 1892.

MERIDEN
Roller Skating Rink.

SPECIAL ATTRACTION
To-morrow Evening

C. C. MARTIN and MISS ALLIE LAWRIE,

The Finest Exhibition Skaters in the Country.

Admission   -   15 cents.

Skates, 10 cents.

1886. ✳SPRING.✳ 1886.
ENTIRE NEW STOCK OF SPRING
✳CLOTHING.✳
MEN'S, BOY'S & CHILDREN'S.
EXCLUSIVE STYLES.
NOBBY PATTERNS.   PERFECT FITTING.
LOWEST PRICES, EVER NAMED.
BOSTON & MERIDEN CLOTHING CO.,
36 COLONY ST., MERIDEN, CONN.

Royal St John
SEWING MACHINE
SPRINGFIELD, Ohio. The only Sewing
Machine in the world
that continues to sew in
the same direction whether
run backward or forward.

Cheshire residents of the 1880s visited area towns and cities for some of their entertainment and shopping needs. These trade cards touted businesses in Meriden. The Meriden Roller Skating Rink was incorporated in 1884 and closed in 1902. C.C. Martin and Allie Lawrie, the finest exhibition skaters in the country, performed sometime during that period. The Boston and Meriden Clothing Company was advertising its entire new stock of spring clothing in this 1886 trade card advertisement. Located at 36 Colony Street, the company featured exclusive styles, nobby patterns, perfect fitting, and the lowest prices ever named. J.F. Ives of 20 Colony Street, in the opera house block, was hoping to sell the Royal St. John sewing machine. His card attracted the reader with a colorful rose; he stamped his name and address on the back.

37

This envelope was addressed to James Lanyon, Esq., the superintendent of the barite mines in Cheshire. Note that it had no street address. The town was still small enough for mail to reach an addressee without a street name. The cancellation reveals it was sent from Simsbury.

TOWN HALL, CHESHIRE, CONN.

Cheshire Town Hall is shown in this 1890 postcard. The structure was erected in 1867 and was already ivy-covered on its north side. The building on the left was located on Foote Street, which ran behind the town hall building.

This is the ornate interior of the Alfred S. Baldwin home, which was located north of what is now the Christ Community Church. The house was the home of Mary Baldwin, namesake of the Mary Baldwin Room in the Cheshire Public Library. It is decorated in the style of the time, c. 1890, and the items in it would probably provoke a bidding frenzy if put up for auction today.

Dr. William T. Foot and his son, John L. Foot, operated a drugstore adjacent to their residence at 29 Wallingford Road. John L. Foot leased the store to H.T. Moss and H.H. Rice in 1890. The doctor was town clerk and the town's first judge of probate. The son was the town's postmaster. When John L. Foot died in 1906, he left an estate of $400,000. Rumors of buried treasure on his property turned out to be true, as a jar containing gold coins was found. That was the extent of the buried treasure found.

Compliments of

→ JOHN · S. · FOOTE ←

MANUFACTURER OF

H. H. RICE'S EC-LEC-TIC LINIMENT & PILLS,

EXT. LEMON, VANILLA AND GINGER

ESS. WINTERGREEN AND PEPPERMINT

Levi S. Peck,
Gen'l Agent.

CHESHIRE, CONN.

John S. Foote was the manufacturer of H.H. Rice's Ec-Lec-Tic Liniment & Pills. According to this card, Levi Peck was listed as the agent. One can only assume it was sold in Moss and Rice's store.

H.T. Moss had his name on the exterior of this store, the former Foot Drugstore. One wonders what happened to H.H. Rice's name. In addition to having quite a large inventory, it was the only gas station in town for a time.

The interior of the Foot Drugstore appeared as it does here c. 1890. The gentlemen in this photograph are identified as Charles Jackson and Tilton Munson. Chocolates were a favorite of the masses even then.

Cheshire's ivy-covered Hull Memorial Baptist Church once occupied the Main Street site on which Christ Community Church is now located. In 1890, Josiah Hull built the church on his own land. He deeded the building and the land to the Baptists. The building was demolished and replaced by the current church in 1966 and 1967.

The Episcopal Academy of Cheshire had its own distinctive stationery and envelopes. This envelope, with its etching of Horton Hall, was sent to Anna Sage of Cromwell on November 16, 1891. The letter it contained was lost, but it is safe to say that it did not address Anna Sage as a student of the academy. Although 117 young women attended the Episcopal Academy in its early years, the last one graduated in 1827. The school did not become coeducational again until 1969.

42

The Ball and Socket Company, of 493 West Main Street, was one of Cheshire's best-known manufacturers and one of its largest employers. Founded in 1850 as the Cheshire Manufacturing Company, it was mainly a button factory, famed for paperweight and cameo buttons. Military buttons were produced during the Civil War, and political buttons were made in the 1890s, especially for the Bryan and McKinley campaigns. In 1901, the company merged with the Ball and Socket Fastener Company of Portsmouth, New Hampshire, and became the Ball and Socket Manufacturing Company. The building still stands, but the company is no longer in existence.

These are some of the buttons that were produced by the Ball and Socket Company. Pres. William McKinley's campaign button is at the top center. To the right of it is Cheshire's bicentennial button.

At one point in its storied existence, Cheshire Academy had a memorabilia room. It was a miniature museum featuring many items of historical significance to the academy. The room no longer exists, although the school has an extensive archive. Items in the academy's collection are available for public viewing during occasional displays that spotlight a specific event or person.

It is not often that a vintage photograph has a specific date attached to it. Sometimes the owner has written the date on the back, but more commonly there is a notation in the caption, for example, "taken around 1890." This photograph does have a specific date: October 28, 1892, the day the Wallace House hotel burned down. The house in the foreground was owned by James Kelsey. It was next door to the conflagration that consumed the hotel. Unfortunately, the Kelseys' home and that of the neighbor next door, Mrs. Martin Brewer in the Abijah Beach House, also suffered some fire damage, but those fires were extinguished before major damage was done. The Abijah Beach House still stands and today is occupied by Dr. and Mrs. Gaudio and family. The Kelsey House, originally built by Samuel Hull c. 1790, is no longer in existence.

In 1796, Prospect was part of Cheshire and was known as Columbia. Methodism was on the rise. After Prospect became a town in 1827, Cheshire Methodists had no local church. This was rectified on November 22, 1834, with the dedication ceremony on land at the corner of Spring Street and Route 10 donated by James Bunnell. Spring Street was known as Bunnell Lane prior to its renaming. Many of the Cornish immigrants employed in the barite mines joined the church. James Lanyon, superintendent of the mines, was prominent among them. The Congregational Society presented the Methodists with their 100-year-old bell in 1891, and it was installed on March 8, 1894. It is housed in the bell tower seen here. The parish moved to the current church, at 205 Academy Road, in 1969. The original building, minus the bell tower, is now the home of Temple Beth David, the town's first synagogue.

Few people realize that the original Cheshire High School was located on the corner of Spring Street and Route 10, in the former Horton residence, and that it was only located there from 1894 to 1911. The 1897 Cheshire High School baseball team appears in a team photograph holding the CHS banner, a few bats, some gloves, and a ball. The boys, from left to right, are as follows: (front row) George Tucker, Herbert Bill, Walter Tucker, and George R. Steele; (middle row) Arthur Bristol, Charles Jackson, and Arthur Woodward; (back row) Irving Guilford, Howard Frost, Nathan Stone, and Clifford Wallace.

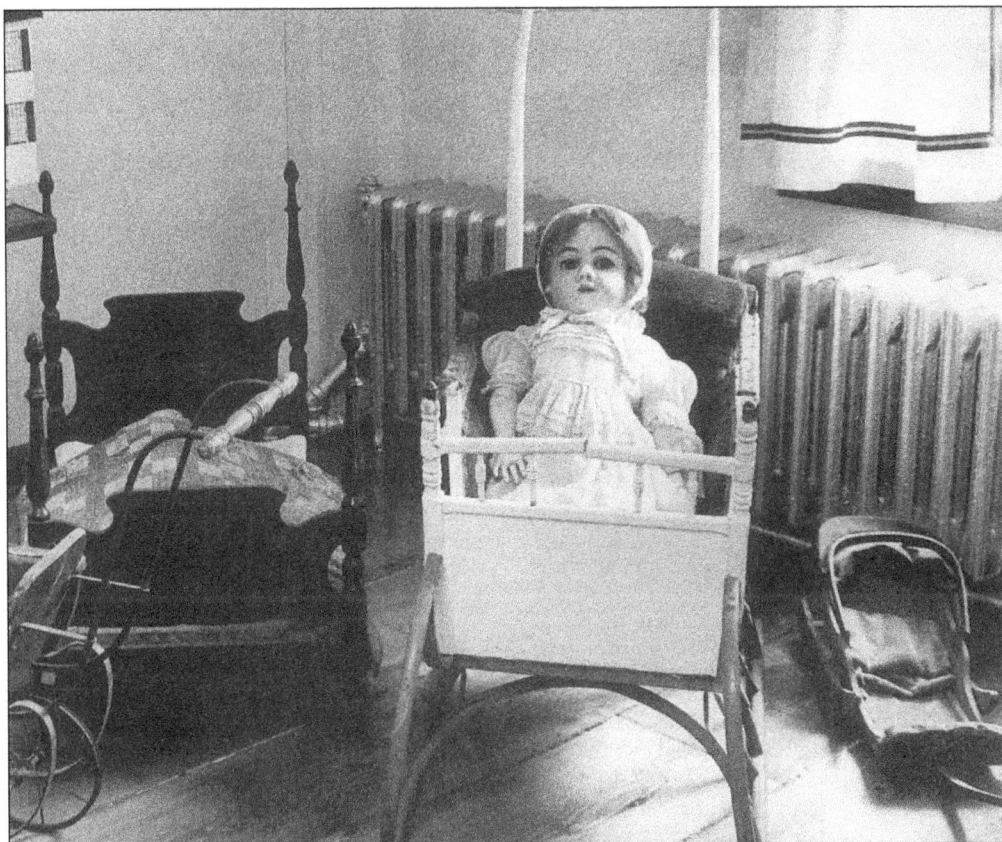

Prominent among its holdings and a favorite with children and adults alike, the Cheshire Historical Society's collection of toys is a prime attraction. These are some of the toys Cheshire's children played with in the 1890s.

The employees of the Armstrong Button Company are gathered for a group photograph in front of the factory on Cheshire Street. Note that all of the men and some of the women are wearing hats, perhaps the precursors of the ubiquitous baseball caps of today.

The Old Brooksvale Post Office was in service from December 28, 1885, through March 19, 1889. Robert Cook was the postmaster for part of that time. The cancellation read "Brooks Vale" when it opened and had changed to the one word, Brooksvale, by the time it closed. This card was issued on May 27, 1962, by the Cheshire Philatelic Society. The years 1860 to 1913 are also listed for the existence of a post office in Brooksvale.

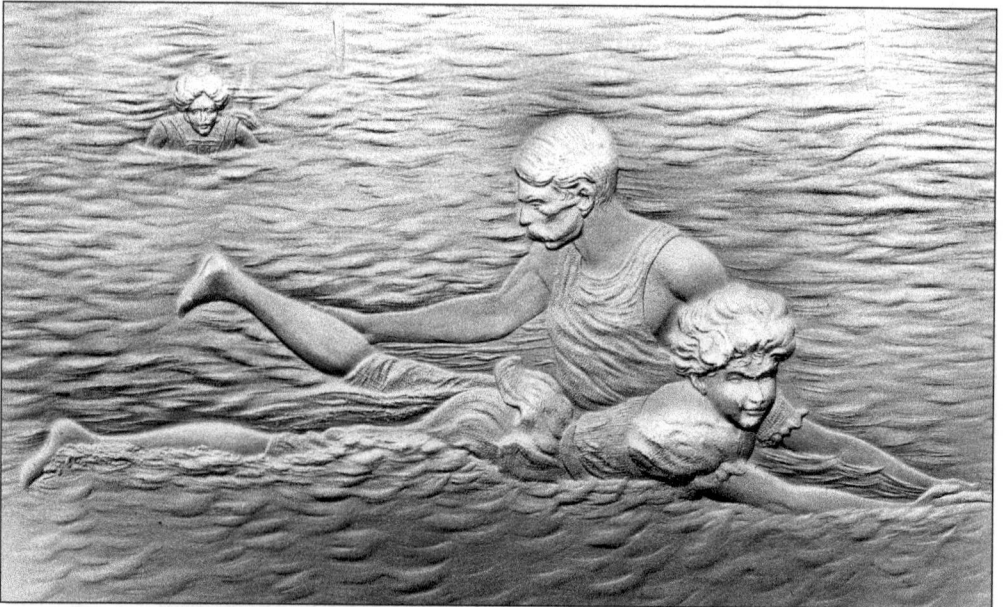

Embossed postcards were very popular for a time. This one portrays the swimmers of the time in appropriate attire. Cheshire swimmers of the period had a few places in town to go to cool off: the old Farmington Canal and Murphy's Pond, now called Mixville Pond and Taylor Pond, were areas to go to beat the heat of the summer sun.

Four

THE DECADE OF
THE OUGHTS

The first decade of the 20th century, the "Decade of the Oughts," found Cheshire more country than town. Farming remained predominant, but manufacturing was still represented. The pace of life in town continued to be relaxed, leaving the hustle and bustle to the city folk beyond Cheshire's borders. In 1905, Cheshire's chapter of the Rotary Club added its name to the town's civic groups.

Scene at Cheshire, Conn

The presence of these couples canoeing on the old Farmington Canal expresses volumes about the pace of life in Cheshire in the 1900s: people with a destination but in no particular hurry to get there.

OLD FLUME RAG HOLLOW CHESHIRE CONN, 451

The Old Flume in Rag Hollow, pictured in this 1900s postcard, is a remnant of the industry that used to operate there. In 1840, the Mix brothers, Titus and John, leased the factory that was located on the second Cheshire lock of the Farmington Canal. They produced kitchen utensils and coffee mills. When the canal closed in 1848, they moved to Rag Hollow, in what is now called Mixville, and founded a company that made clay dress buttons, bits, gimlets, and augurs. The Mix Manufacturing Company harnessed the water's power to turn machinery to polish its products.

UNITED STATES OF AMERICA REPLY CARD

THIS SIDE IS FOR THE ADDRESS ONLY.

POSTAGE
1831 SHERIDAN 1888
ONE CENT

M. A. TRAVIS, Supt.

Beechwood Dairy,

Irvington, N. Y.

Marketing by mail was common, even in the early years of the new century. The U.S. Postal Service issued these business reply postal cards in 1904 for use by companies and their customers to communicate with each other. Cheshire residents of the period saw this profile of Gen. Philip H. Sheridan on the one-cent card.

50

This 1900s postcard shows the home of Alexander Doolittle, in Brooksvale, originally built in 1784 by Jerre Brooks. Alexander Doolittle was the grandson of Amos Doolittle, the well-known Cheshire artist who drew scenes of the initial battles of the Revolutionary War at Lexington and Concord. Copies of the drawings (based on the paintings of Ralph Earl) are on display at the Cheshire Historical Society. Jerre Brooks was the grandson of Thomas Brooks, the man who gave New Cheshire its name.

The Old Canal, Brooksvale, Conn.

A wide part of the abandoned Farmington Canal is pictured in this c. 1905 postcard of Brooksvale. Canoeing, swimming, and fishing were popular leisure time activities in this area of the old canal.

It is 1905, and you are in the center of town in front of Cheshire Academy's Bowden Hall, in an uncharacteristic hurry to get to the railroad station on West Main Street. Yelling "Hey, taxi," probably would not have helped. This gentleman, with his stylish surrey and stalwart steed, would have been your best bet. He is Mr. Peters, and one of his jobs was to serve as the town cabby. He was also an employee of Edgar Beadle, owner of a wagon shop on the corner of Main Street and the part of Route 10 that is now called Highland Avenue.

E.W. Hazard of Southington was a professional photographer who, judging from the large number of photographs by him, spent a lot of time in Cheshire. This c. 1907 panoramic view was taken from the railroad tracks looking westward up West Main Street. The shot shows the station on the left, where Ye Old Station Auto Body is now. The Cheshire Provision Company

Mr. Peters, the town cabby, would drive his passengers westward, down West Main Street, to catch the train. This is a view looking in the direction of the railroad station, located at the bottom of the hill.

is located on the right, on the property now owned by the Lyon and Billard Lumber Company. The train is just pulling into the station. Look closely and you will see a family peering out of the carriage, preparing to shop at the Cheshire Provision Company.

The left side of this panoramic postcard by E.W. Hazard looks eastward, up West Main Street, toward the corner of Maple Avenue. The building behind the tree was part of the Ball and Socket Manufacturing Company's complex but is no longer in existence. The right side of

P.J. Ethers owned this store in West Cheshire. This real photo postcard bears a 7:00 p.m., February 3, 1909 cancellation from the West Cheshire Post Office. Closer examination with a magnifying lens reveals signs directing travelers to New Haven, Hartford, Boston, and New York. The shopkeeper, possibly P.J. Ethers himself, can be seen in back of a sidewalk sign promoting the sale of ice cream. This photograph was probably taken in the month of July.

Hazard's panoramic faces southward down the railroad tracks adjacent to the Ball and Socket factory. The railroad station seen at the bottom of page 52 is pictured again on the far right of the card.

The Porter and Welton store was located on the east side of Main Street (now called Route 10 or South Main Street) almost directly opposite where Cornwall Avenue enters the main street. The operators sold groceries and dry goods, and the store later became an A & P grocery. The building has seen a succession of businesses and additions over the years. It is currently occupied by California Nails.

J.R. Bishop and his assistant are seen boiling spray mixture for the fruit trees on the farm in this May 13, 1907 photograph. Bishop Farms is still located at 500 South Meriden Road but is now owned by the Romanik family and features a gift store, farm store, and winery.

Labeled in this photograph as Judge Bronson's Summer Cottage, the building was eventually purchased by Walter Scott, owner of the Waverly Inn, which was located a few blocks south along Maple Avenue. The building is a commercial property today, located on the corner of Park Place and Maple Avenue.

The Cheshire Green has always been a magnet for town celebrations and events. Residents were treated to a carnival there in August 1907. Some of the carnival tents can be seen in this photograph, one of them bedecked with an American flag.

Blonden was a famous tightrope walker who appeared at a carnival at Walter Scott's Waverly Inn in 1909. He was one of the early performers to be known by only one name.

The Casino was a popular gathering spot for area revelers. It was owned by local hosteler Walter Scott, and this card establishes it as the "Ladies & gents annex of the Waverly Inn." This printed statement was important to the research for this book because local historians had long held that this building was, in fact, the Shelter, which was actually located across the street. This card established the link to the Waverly Inn and helped to confirm the author's contention that the Casino became the Waverly (probably after the 1912 fire destroyed the earlier version of the Waverly located just up the street).

The area around the corner of Hinman Road and Maple Avenue was called Scott's Junction, undoubtedly because Walter Scott owned most of the nearby property. This panoramic photo postcard was published by Alfred V. Oxley of Southington but was probably taken by E.W. Hazard. The building in the center is the Casino. Note what appears to be a statue of a white

The interior of the Casino had pool tables and an extensive bar. Customers probably played cards here, but it was not what people would consider the casino of today.

dog on the lawn of the Casino. The building on the right is the Waverly Inn that burned down in 1912. The picture was taken facing eastward from in front of the Shelter, a popular place to buy a soda and to wait for the trolley. The trolley tracks were torn up c. 1937 and a former resident maintains the scrap metal was sold to Japan.

This photograph was taken from the center of what is now South Main Street when it was still unpaved. E.W. Hazard was facing northward when he snapped the photograph. In the far left of the image is the stable for the First Congregational Church. Note the trolley tracks and the sign on the telephone pole that proclaims "Cars Stop Here #48." The Cheshire Town Hall

Strolling a bit farther north, this is the scene E.W. Hazard encountered. Cheshire High School is the second building on the left toward the west. That building was replaced in 1912 by what is now Humiston School, home to the department of education, adult education, and

has a front porch complete with pillars. Also, there is no white marble fountain in front of the building. The fountain, which provided water for people on the sidewalk side and horses on the street side, did not appear until 1912.

other programs. The homes in the center of the picture are still in existence and are owned by Cheshire Academy. Horton Hall, which burned down in 1941, is the large building directly behind the boy on the bicycle. Bowden and Bronson Halls are at the far right.

Proceeding northward, the casual stroller gets a little closer look at the architecture of the first version of Cheshire High School and of St. Peter's Church, on the left side of the postcard. Horton Hall dominates the right side of this photograph of Main Street. Look closely just in

Behind Horton and Bronson Hall, tennis enthusiasts are prowling the courts. A twin water tower with its wind-powered, rotating vanes is also visible in the background of the

front of Horton Hall to see the corner of the road that was eventually abandoned, filled in, and covered with grass.

photograph on page 65. The Methodist church and Cheshire High School are seen to the right of Horton Hall.

Leaving the tennis courts, continuing southward along Elm Street, and then turning eastward down Wallingford Road brings the intrepid explorer of central Cheshire to the front of the Durand family home. Some of the family members are standing outside. The home is currently owned by Laraine Smith. Across the street is the Independent Order of Odd Fellows (IOOF)

Arriving at the top of the hill and facing eastward, looking down Wallingford Road, the side of Cheshire Town Hall is visible on the left. A block or so down the road is the Durand cottage, the building that had to be moved from the green in 1826 to make way for the First Congregational Church edifice. The Durand cottage has since been replaced by another structure. The large house on the corner is the Deacon E.R. Brown residence. It was the home

Hall, now the home of Changing Seasons Early Learning Center. The unique double water tower from page 62 is seen in the background. The building on the right is Seabury Hall, now the home of the Watch Factory Shoppes. Looking west up the hill is Brown's Corner, where E.W. Hazard took the next photograph in the series.

to the first two presidents of the Episcopal Academy. E.R. Brown is the coauthor of *Old Historic Homes of Cheshire*, published in 1895, and is one of the founders of the Cheshire Watch Factory. The photograph at the bottom of page 75 is a view of the same house from the front and probably depicts Edwin R. Brown himself, viewing a parade with family and friends.

The next photograph in the series shows the same corner from a bit farther north on South Main Street. The scene includes a view down Foote Street, which is no longer in existence,

Just a little farther south from Brown's Corner is the Squire Beach House. In 1986, this building was uprooted, rotated, and moved back from the road. It became a restaurant and is now R.P. Downey's. The Governor Foote House, now the First Union Bank, is in the center of the

and trolley tracks. The buildings around the green, including the First Congregational Church, are featured in this half of the postcard.

photograph, where Cornwall Avenue intersects what was then called Main Street but what is now called South Main Street. Dr. Cornwall's house occupies most of the right side of the postcard. The wall was subsequently removed, and the building is now a commercial property.

Main Street.
Cheshire Conn.

Continuing southward, this close-up of the Squire Beach House is labeled Main Street because that is what the road was called in 1908—the cancellation date on the back of the card. Samuel Beach built the house on the left in 1762. He was a lawyer and served in the Connecticut state legislature. Beach, Reuben Atwater, and John Peck represented the townspeople in their successful attempt to become a town in 1780. Samuel Beach's son, Burrage Beach, was also a lawyer and lived in the house until his death in 1894. He was one of the directors of the Farmington Canal, serving with the famous inventor Eli Whitney from Hamden. The Governor Foote House can be seen across the street on the corner of Cornwall Avenue.

Main Street Cheshire, Conn.

Turning northward from the same area, the viewer sees the Cook House on the west side of the street and commercial establishments on the east side. The sign with the horse head picture reads "Horse Shoeing W.C. Dailey."

Five

A WARM SPOT THROUGH THE TEENS

The decade from 1910 through 1919 was an eventful one in Cheshire and in the world beyond its borders. The Lady Fenwick Chapter of the Daughters of the American Revolution was founded in 1910. Mary Baldwin moved the library from her house to the Williams House, on Main Street, in 1911. Humiston School opened, and Beach's *History of Cheshire 1694–1840* was published. The Cheshire Fire Department was founded, R.W. Hine began his hardware store, and the Waverly Inn burned down in 1912. The Cheshire Reformatory opened and the York Hill Trap Rock Company started quarrying in West Cheshire. Some of Cheshire's young men went off to fight in World War I. More than 100 of them served, and six were killed in action. Two women also served: a nurse and a yeoman. The local branch of the American Red Cross, led by Nettie Smith, and the Boy Scouts and Girl Scouts were organized in 1917. Amazingly, a Virginia company drilled a wildcat oil well near what is now Dodd Middle School. The oil well did not pan out.

A Dutch couple proclaim their love for Cheshire.

Old barns have a way of leaving a lover of rustic scenes with a warm feeling. This venerable, old Cheshire barn was one of many located throughout this farming community. It is quite possible it was made of chestnut wood, the wood of choice for many such structures before the blight killed off the trees. This photograph was taken by local lensman J. Michael Johnson.

The trains of the Meriden, Waterbury, and Connecticut River Line crossed the trestle at the Notch in West Cheshire, on their way up the steep grade to Waterbury. The trolley line's tracks ran under the trestle.

The Cheshire Reformatory was completed in 1912. For the most part, it has been a good neighbor; it used to be the town's movie theatre. Residents and inmates watched movies together on Friday nights. It is an imposing structure, set far back from Route 10 at the end of a long, tree-lined driveway.

The Moss Mill Pond used to be called the Old Swimming Hole. It was purchased by Walter Percival, who turned it into a showplace, replete with classical sculpture and stone walls. This postcard is one of a set issued by the Cheshire Historical Society during the U.S. bicentennial celebration of 1976.

Judging by the size of his Foote Street home, Dr. Karrmann was undoubtedly a wealthy citizen of Cheshire. However, little is known about him.

Foote Street used to connect Wallingford Road with South Main Street, running in back of the old town hall. Houses were torn down and the road was paved over to make way for the Cheshire Town Hall addition that was completed in 1989. Identified in this picture are Henry Beadle (left) and Willie, standing in front of Sam Wah's Laundry.

Cheshire Academy, old Building, Cheshire, Conn.

Many well-known individuals have walked the grounds of Cheshire Academy including Gideon Welles, secretary of the navy under Pres. Abraham Lincoln; Joseph Wheeler, a future Confederate cavalry general; and J.P. Morgan, a wealthy financier.

Cheshire, Conn. Cheshire Green.

The sentinel spire of the gleaming white First Congregational Church watches over the green. Many residents believe it is the town green, but it is actually owned by the church; so, it is rightfully the church green. Designed by prominent architect David Hoadley and built in 1826 and 1827, the church originally cost $6,872.59. Its spire has become a symbol of Cheshire and appears in the town seal.

74

Formerly the home of the Rev. Sanford J. Horton, principal of the Episcopal Academy, this building once housed Cheshire's first high school for a few years. However, the school lost its accreditation. After eight graduating classes, it became a graded school. In 1911, Julia Humiston pledged $30,000 to the town with the stipulation that a new school be built on the Horton site and be named after her father, Daniel Humiston. This came to pass in 1912. The children and teachers in this photograph remain unidentified.

Main Street curves past Horton Hall. Three boys are playing in the dirt road, which is a major thoroughfare today.

Another view of Horton Hall reveals its imposing size. The building and the road on its side no longer exist.

CHESHIRE MILITARY ACADEMY, CHESHIRE, CONN.

A sporty car of the era is parked outside of Horton Hall. The caption is worth closer scrutiny. It calls the school Cheshire Military Academy. The postcard publisher must have labeled it incorrectly. Ann Moriarity, current archivist for the academy, maintains that at no time during its proud history was the school ever officially called Cheshire Military Academy.

"The Grand Old Man of Cheeshire" is what Eri Davidson Woodbury was called in his obituary. The misspelling of Cheshire appeared in a 1928 Associated Press obituary for the Cheshire resident. He was the town's last surviving veteran of the Civil War. He was known for having single-handedly captured the colors of the 12th North Carolina Infantry at the battle of Cedar Creek, for which he was awarded the Congressional Medal of Honor. He was wounded the night before Lee's surrender, losing a finger in the experience. He served as headmaster of the Episcopal Academy of Connecticut. His grave is located behind St. Peter's Episcopal Church, and Woodbury Court bears his name. Woodbury died at his home at the age of 90.

Ives Corner is located at the intersection of Cook Hill Road, Harrison Road, and South Brooksvale Road. Elmer Ives ran a small store on the corner called "The Why Not Rest: A Good Place to Shop." He stocked cigarettes, cigars, tobacco, soda, and candy. The store doubled as a trolley freight station. This photograph, published as a postcard for the 1976 bicentennial, shows William Judd and Mrs. Perkins, both residents of Harrison Road. The tiny building was demolished by an out-of-control car in 1953.

Another postcard in the Cheshire Historical Society's 1976 reprint series is this view of the bridge at the foot of Cheshire Street. It also features a view of the trestle of the Meriden, Waterbury, and Connecticut River Railroad.

RESIDENCE OF E.R. BROWN CHESHIRE CT JULY 4TH 1911

Parades are important to the fiscal and historical health of a community. They are a live-action inventory and decorated display of a municipality's civic groups, businesses, beauty queens, student clubs, sports teams, and bands. Parades are a form of mobile communication in which local, state, and, sometimes, national public servants and politicians participate as a way of informing their constituents that they are still around, are active, and are accessible. Parades are giant three-dimensional billboards that advertise for new members, clients, or customers and that express the vitality of the community. Around the periphery of the parade, among the spectators, area entrepreneurs are able to sell their wares. The spectators, especially families, have the added benefit of spending a few hours of quality time together.

E.W. Hazard was a tireless recorder of Cheshire life. He covered the 1911 and 1912 Independence Day parades in an extensive series of photographs. The exact amount of exposures at each event is not known, but the numbers in the corners go up into the 40s. Some of the postcards can be found in Cheshire collections, but this is probably the first time since Hazard took the photographs that so many have appeared in one place. They have been gathered primarily from four collections: the Cheshire Historical Society's, Ralph Edson's, Judge Ray Voelker's, and the author's.

Deacon E.R. Brown decorated his house and invited family and friends over to view the 1911 Fourth of July parade from his prime vantage on the corner of Wallingford Road and South Main Street. He was a prominent local businessman and expert on Cheshire History, co-author with J.R. Paddock of *Old Historic Homes of Cheshire*, which is one of the primary sources of information for this book. Brown operated a store farther down South Main Street beginning in 1871. This building and the one next to it, which had belonged to Nettie Smith of the Cheshire Red Cross, were victims of a wrecking ball in 1970 that made the way for the commercial shops now called Cheshire Center.

LADY FENWICK CHAPTER D.A.R. CHESHIRE CT JULY 4th 1911.
THIS WAGON USED DURING WAR OF 1812.   HAZARD' PHOTO

The Lady Fenwick Chapter members of the Daughters of the American Revolution are dressed in their patriotic finery, accompanied by young men in tricornered hats in a horse-drawn wagon. This wagon was used in the War of 1812. The wagon section, minus the wheels and axles, is stored in a barn on the Baldwin-Johnson property to this day.

GRANGE WAGON CHESHIRE CONN JULY 4th 1911.
BY HAZARD.

Festooned with crops and plants and carrying what appears to be a model of a well, the Cheshire Grange wagon, with its fine crop of farm families, passes by the town hall.

Surely one of the parade's most highly decorated and patriotic floats, the Cheshire School Children C.S.R. team passes by Wallingford Road. (The meaning of the initials is unknown.) The float is proceeding in a northerly direction while some participants are going in a southerly direction. The reason for this is unclear.

The parade marshal and his aides ride regally along while being observed by two Cheshire youths perched on the roof of the town hall's front porch.

The South East District's team leaves Church Drive, pulled by four white horses. It must have been a scorcher on parade day in 1911; umbrellas seemed to be the order of the day on many of the floats. South East District probably refers to one of the town's schools. Interestingly, the "So." has been left out on another version of this postcard.

A replica of the Liberty Bell rests on this flag-filled float. The wheels are covered by what appear to be strands of bundled hay.

The Peasely Pony Cart takes its turn emerging from Church Drive to join the other floats. Note the sign hanging off the tree. It advertises F.L. Rice's Livery and Feed Stable. The two youths are still perched precariously on the porch roof, and it is now possible to clearly see the family standing on the porch viewing the parade.

The Cheshire Fire Department was officially organized in 1912. This photograph is entitled "Chief of Fire Department, Cheshire CT, July 4, 1911." The man wearing the fireman's hat is carrying a fireman's trumpet filled with flowers. His hat has the number 1 on the front of it, so it is safe to assume he is the chief. The driver of the car is sitting in a vehicle with the steering wheel located on the right side. The location of the steering wheel on the left side of cars had not yet been standardized.

One of the jewels of E.W. Hazard's entire collection is this portrait of a man proudly posing in front of his family-filled automobile. Surely one could not refer to such a vehicle as a mere car. This, truly, is an automobile. The man posing to the rear of the vehicle is Walter Scott. He was named after the famed writer and has been featured prominently in this book as the owner of the Waverly Inn and the Casino. Note the post behind Scott. It looks as if a man is holding a ventriloquist's dummy atop the post. It is actually a real boy standing farther back, but made to look positioned on the post by chance. You should recognize this image as the one that may have originally drawn your attention to the front of this book. It is the image that graces the cover. A "cover boy" after all these years, Walter Scott, promoter that he was, would have been ecstatic.

The Old Washington Chaise was another of Walter Scott's possessions, and he used it to promote his restaurant by displaying it in front of the Waverly Inn and in town parades. The man costumed as Gen. George Washington cut a fine figure, as his driver guided the chaise along the 1911 parade route. A close-up can be seen on page 98.

This photo postcard is number 40 in E.W. Hazard's offerings in the 1912 Independence Day parade series. It appears first in order to draw the viewer into the crowd of onlookers, as if it were possible to be among them. Look closely at the faces, many of which are filled with anticipation. There is a photographer among them. Could it be Hazard, his image captured by his assistant using another camera? The bunting-draped monument in the background is the one in the center of the green. It stands today and is reputed to be the first Civil War monument erected in the state, in 1866. It was designed by Robert W. Wright of New Haven and cost over $2,000.

Labeled "Indian Float" and carrying a tepee and a few Native Americans, these wagons seem to be in an area other than the green.

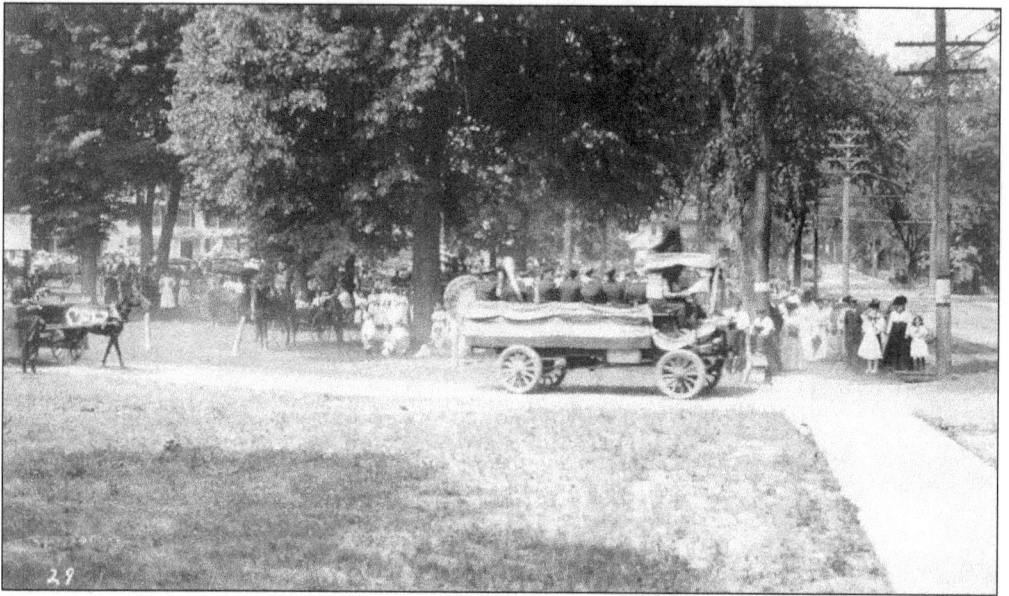

Number 29 in the series, this card is labeled "Cheshire Band" and shows the band about to exit Church Drive, immediately followed by the Cheshire Fire Department float. However, the next photograph (below) that was snapped is numbered with a 7 in the lower left corner. Apparently the images were not always numbered consecutively. Perhaps the numbers were arbitrarily assigned in the darkroom.

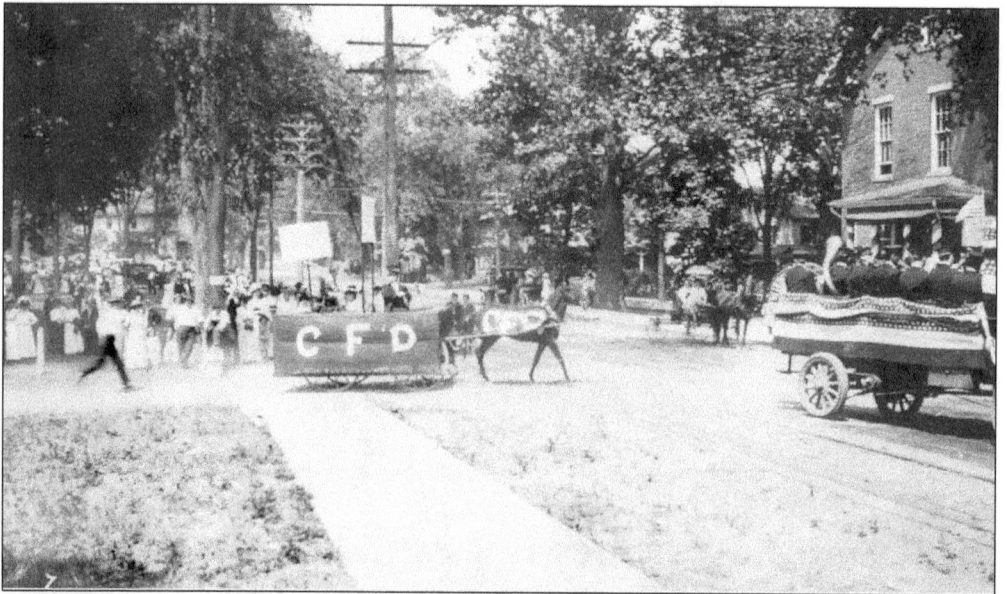

The Cheshire Fire Department (C.F.D.) appears to have a very small float. Based on another card in the series, a contingent of firemen probably marched in back of the wagon. The back of the card reveals that Irving Guilford and Dick Williams planned the parade and that the horse is named Black Beauty and belongs to Williams.

The year 1912 brought with it a new look for the Cheshire Grange's wagon; lots of bunting and a maypole-style tent effect gave their float a more patriotic look than the more earthy float of the year before. This image must have been taken shortly before or after the one on the bottom of page 86. The umbrella-topped carriage is still in the same spot in front of the Cheshire Town Hall.

One of the wagons carrying schoolchildren in 1912 contains about 20 youngsters, bunting, plants, and American flags. In E.W. Hazard's photograph, the wagon is leaving Church Drive, crossing the trolley tracks in front of the town hall, and heading southward.

Back again in 1912, the Peasley Pony Cart carries the three girls, most likely members of the Peasley family, northward along the parade route.

Undoubtedly taken within a few moments of the previous photo postcard (the couple viewing the parade from their front porch is in the same position) this one is entitled "Count & Countess Rochambeau." The man and woman riding in the cart have gone to great lengths to duplicate the look of the historical couple.

Another view taken from the same vantage point and at around the same time, this card features "Lady Riders." No additional identification is made. These women might just be a group of friends who share a common love of riding, or they might be part of an actual organization devoted to horseback riding.

The men of the Cheshire Fire Department appear in the 1912 parade pulling the fire department's water wagon. It is likely that the department's first chief, Paul Klimpke, is leading the group, but this is not verified on the card.

These "Men Riders," about to enter the parade from Church Drive, may be the parade marshal and his aides shown in other E.W. Hazard shots. Other wagons and carts can be seen lining up in front of the Hitchcock-Phillips House, preparing to join the parade.

Just before or just after participating in the 1912 Independence Day parade, these riders are flanked by interested onlookers.

The parade marshal and his aides are pictured parading in front of the Casino on July 4, 1912. A puzzling aspect of this photograph is the position of the Casino building so close to the street. In most other pictures featuring this structure, it appears to be much farther back from Maple Avenue.

In 1912, women had not yet gained the right to vote. Cheshire had a vocal and demonstrative group of suffragettes who chose the public forum of the Independence Day Parade to make their case to the captive audience of fellow townspeople lining the parade route.

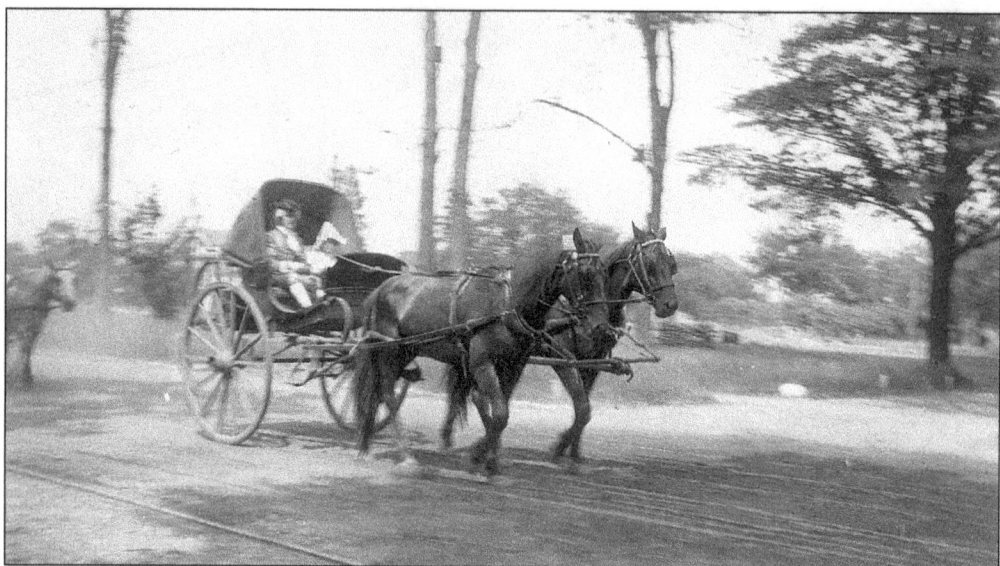

Walter Scott's George Washington Chaise is in the parade again in 1912. "George Washington" seems to be the same person who rode in the parade last year, but his passenger is a small child this year, probably a young girl.

The "Hunters Float" carries four men, three of whom display firearms. A small boy is perched in the back, wearing a feathered headdress. The buck's head, with its impressive rack of antlers, certainly makes a stately hood ornament.

A wagon containing a group of schoolchildren proceeds in a southerly direction, past the town hall, toward the E.R. Brown residence on South Main Street. The youngsters are wearing what appear to be dunce caps. It is highly unlikely, however, that such a negative practice would have been represented in such a positive event as a parade.

The men and women on this wagon are projecting a mixed message. There appears to be a small cannon mounted on the back of the float. There is a large spinning wheel with a few women seated in front of it. The wagon wheels and sides are decorated with bunting and large paper flowers.

E.W. Hazard of Southington was a prominent photographer of the early part of the 20th century. He was well known for his shots of parades, events, and panoramic street scenes. This photograph is captioned "No. 4 The First Car & Passengers over the Waterbury & Milldale Line." This original photograph from the author's collection has "G.S. Alling, 22 Carlson St., New Britain, Conn." stamped on its cardboard backing. G.S. Alling may be one of the dignitaries in the shot, but none of the 27 men and one dog is identified. The picture may not even have been taken in Cheshire, but this car is definitely one that passed through Cheshire carrying local residents to area locations.

Cheshire trolley riders on their way to Waterbury were treated to this view of a huge tree growing atop a large boulder. The startling sight was located on Cheshire Road in Waterbury and is no longer in existence.

A group of people waits for the trolley in front of the Shelter on Maple Avenue. The trolley is approaching from the south. The card was published by Oxley Stores in Southington, but the photograph itself was probably taken by E.W. Hazard. Standing in front of the Shelter, these

This photo postcard and the one above it are owned by Warren S. Jones, a former Cheshire resident who now lives in Texas. It is labeled "Scott's Junction" and is taken from a different vantage than the one on page 58. This one was taken from about the position of the trolley in the postcard above it on this page. It was actually the first concrete verification of the author's contention that the Shelter and the Casino were not the same building. Some local historians

women look as if they are waiting for a fashion show instead of a trolley. The Shelter was owned by the McClearys, and it had a soda fountain inside. The bend in the tracks may be caused by a trick of the camera lens.

had steadfastly maintained that they were the same building. This is the only known photograph that shows both establishments simultaneously, proving they were distinct structures. The Shelter is the second building on the left side of the card. The Casino, with a distinctive gazebo out front, is the building on the far right.

This close-up of the Casino features a sign touting the Eagle Brewing Company's ales, lager, and porter.

This chaise was imported from England in 1702 and was reputed to be the oldest carriage in the world on its own wheels. Owned by Walter Scott, it was displayed at the Waverly Inn and was sometimes ridden in parades. Unfortunately, it was destroyed in a fire. George Washington is said to have ridden in it from Middletown to Wethersfield.

WAVERLY INN, ON COLLEGE HIGHWAY, CHESHIRE, CONN.

The Casino eventually became the Waverly Inn. The building is pictured here later in its existence, with additions.

The Shelter, located across the street from the Casino, is highlighted in this close-up. The chairs on the deck of this soda shop and trolley stop can be seen, as well as what appears to be a sidewalk scale.

This is the version of Walter Scott's Waverly Inn that burned down in 1912.

A shot of the same building, but from across the street, shows the distinctive white gazebo located in front of the Casino. This card helped to convince local historians that the building was not a different version of the Casino building, thus clearing up another of the many mysteries regarding the identities of the Shelter, the Casino, and the Waverly Inn.

The remaining unsolved mystery regarding the Waverly Inn is shown in the captions of the two postcards on this page. The card above states "Martin's Waverly Inn, Cheshire, Conn." No one can remember any connection with an owner named Martin.

This photograph, apparently taken around the same time, showing the same line of rocks used for the curb, is captioned, "The Waverly, Walter Scott, Innkeeper, Cheshire, Conn."

A Cheshire family, not representing any group or organization, covered their car in a profusion of pompoms, patriotic stars, stripes, and American flags. The back of the card reveals an interesting coincidence. One of the women in the car wrote the message and signed it "Sarah," with no last name. The message began, "This is our car as it looked in the July 4th Parade." It is dated July 21, 1916, and is addressed to Louise Whiting, Wilson's Cottages, Jackson, New Hampshire.

The Cheshire Fire Department was well represented in the Fourth of July parade of 1916. The five members of the group are riding in what may be the town's first fire truck. It is pulling equipment, including a rolled-up hose.

Another wagon that looks like it participated in the 1916 Fourth of July parade is parked in front of 25 Church Drive. Lettered on the side and barely visible on the original photograph postcard is "Trolley Express Co." It is not clear what bunting-covered cargo is on the wagon.

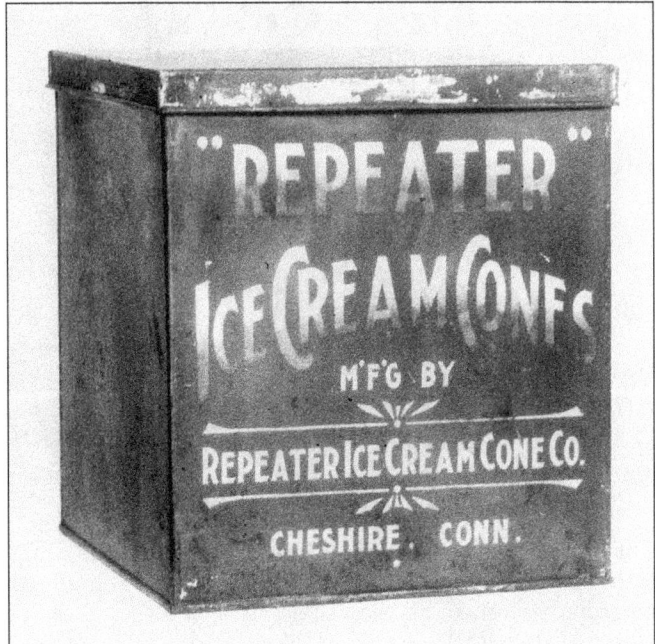

The Repeater Ice Cream Cone Company was located across from the green and turned out "mighty tasty cones," according to an elderly resident who sampled them as a child. The company was in business for about a decade beginning c. 1915. The metal box in the photograph was used to store the stacked cones to keep them fresh. One of the original boxes is on display at Sweet Claude's Ice Cream Parlor on South Main Street in Cheshire.

THE
CRESCENT

This pen-and-ink drawing of a soldier embracing a Red Cross nurse evokes the bittersweet emotions of wartime. It appeared on the June 1917 cover of *The Crescent*, a literary magazine published by the Alpha Chapter of Gamma Delta Psi in the interest of New Haven High School.

The American flag still flies today, thanks to the patriots who fought in World War I.

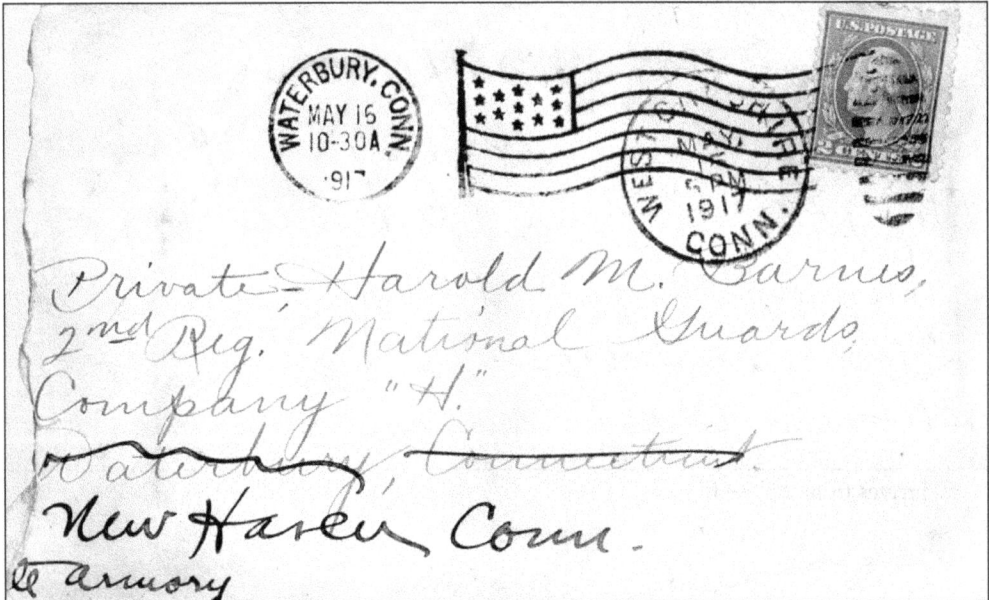

Private Harold M. Barnes,
2nd Reg. National Guards,
Company "H."
~~Waterbury, Connecticut.~~
New Haven Conn.
2e armory

One of the Cheshire residents who defended our country was Pvt. Harold M. Barnes, 2nd Regiment National Guard, Company H. Imagine you are a lonely soldier, having just left home for training. You look forward to a letter from home and . . . "Mail call!"

Cheshire, Conn.
May 19, 1917.

My dear Harold:

How are you
getting along?

Did you receive
my letter? Thought
you would drop a
few lines at least.
Quet sent us a card.
I am writing him
also to-day.

Tom Kelly over
here, you know the
Shipping Clerk enlisted
Thursday night. He
goes to New Haven

News arrives from a close relative.

Do you see Walter
every day. Hope so.
Now take good
care of yourself. Get
plenty of sleep
Hoping to hear
from you very soon
I remain as ever.
With lots of love from
all. Your loving sister
Ethel

P.S. Do not suppose
you will get this
until Monday.

A "loving sister" named Ethel, back home on Maple Avenue in Cheshire, sends "lots of love."

Cheshire Town Hall in 1918 has a different look to the front porch, which is more ornate than the previous one. The water fountain is now installed. The Red Cross chapter meets downstairs. The white flag with the red cross on it can be seen in the lower right corner.

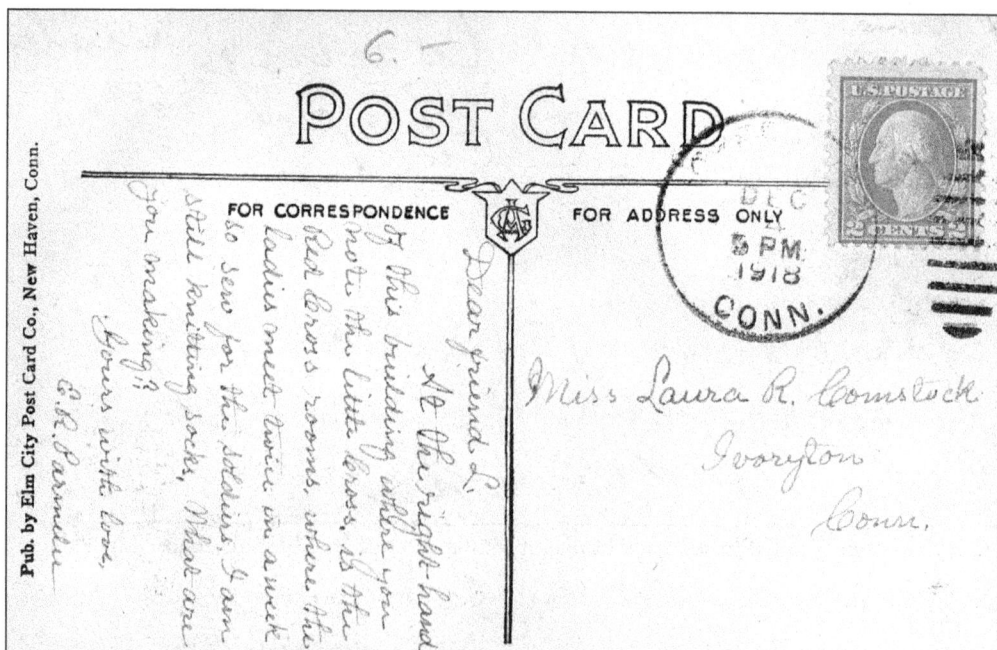

E.R. Parmelee addresses a message to her friend Laura Comstock of Ivoryton on December 4, 1918. She meets with other like-minded volunteers to sew and knit for the soldiers. Knitted socks are her specialty. This is the back of the postcard above.

Humiston School is visible on the west side of Main Street, near the intersection with Academy Road.

Roxbury Tutoring School, Cheshire, Conn.

Horton Hall is located nearby on the east side of Main Street. The postcard is labeled Roxbury Tutoring School, although that was never the official name of the school.

This is another view of Main Street (now South Main Street or Route 10) looking northward toward Horton Hall.

Woodbridge Hall, once located on Academy Road, was part of Roxbury School.

110

Six

A Time of Plenty in the Twenties

While the twenties were roaring elsewhere, life was relatively calm in Cheshire. There was still plenty going on, though. The R.A. Storrs Post of the American Legion was founded in 1920. The First Congregational Church celebrated its 200th anniversary on September 13, 1924, with a series of reenactments tracing the history of the United States. An addition was built on Humiston School, and the last train ran on the Canal Line in 1925. Cohen's Department Store opened on October 9, 1926. The town continued to host travelers and revelers in a number of taverns, hotels, and inns.

A group of commercial properties is featured on this postcard. Now called the Plaza Block—and the "Alamo" by some, because of the angular facades on the buildings—this active business area is located where Main Street intersects West Main Street. The gas station sign in the center has Socony lettered on it.

The Maplewood Hotel on West Main Street was a popular place to stay. Other businesses eventually occupied its neatly kept rooms. Today, the site is home to Rossini's Restaurant.

The Coach Lamp Inn
CHESHIRE · CONN.

Mildred Brannian operated the Coach Lamp Inn, represented on this postcard. Originally built in 1768, it is a fine example of early American Colonial architecture. The advertisement on the back of the card informed the reader that it was open all year for luncheon, tea, and dinner. It was located in the Ives Corner area, on the College Highway, which is yet another name for Route 10.

DOG-TEAM TEA HOUSE CHESHIRE, CONNECTICUT
GRENFELL LABRADOR INDUSTRIES

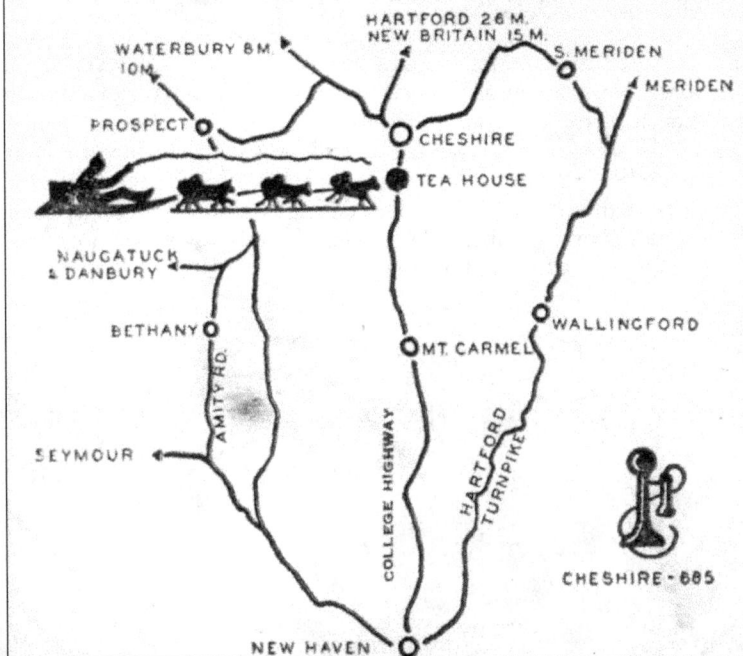

The Dog Team Tea House not only possesses a unique and memorable name, it has a fascinating history. The map on the front of the card places it a few miles from the center of town, on the College Highway. The back of the card reveals that it is operated by the Grenfell Labrador Industries to benefit Sir Wilfred Grenfell's Labrador work. It turns out that Grenfell was a well-known doctor who practiced among the Eskimos and seamen in Labrador and was responsible for starting and helping to maintain Labrador's hospitals. Grenfell is even listed in encyclopedias. He was knighted in 1927, and his supporters in the United States, England, and Canada formed the International Grenfell Association, setting up hundreds of outlets such as Cheshire's Dog Team Tea House to raise money. Surprisingly, he has a distant relative in Cheshire who did not know that one of Grenfell's Dog Team Tea Houses was located in his hometown. The association is still in existence today, headquartered in Newfoundland.

The Rufus Hitchcock Store began as a grocery store in 1787. It continued operating in the same location, 7 South Main Street, for 188 years, until 1975. Hotchkiss, Allen, and then Mr. Munger operated it for some of those years. The store was purchased by the Platt brothers in 1914. They sold it in 1947. The photograph on page 12 of *Landmarks of Old Cheshire* shows a picture of the interior that is incorrectly labeled "*c.* 1910." It was actually dated September 1939. The exterior shot above, numbered 17, is part of a series, as are number 21, the curve on Main Street, which appears below, and number 23, the town hall, which appears on page 115.

This is another view of the curve on Main Street. The Methodist church and Humiston School can be seen on the right. The Platt Brothers Store is located farther down, beyond the house with the shutters.

TOWN HALL, CHESHIRE, CONN. 23.

Number 23 in the series depicts the Cheshire Town Hall in all its magnificence, replete with the four Ionic columns on its front porch, the beautiful marble water fountain, and the year 1867, when it was approved, in brick above the topmost windows. The Cheshire Town Hall was authorized at a town meeting in February 1867 and was officially opened on January 1, 1868. The opening was celebrated with a New Year's Eve ball. There was an abundance of room in the spacious building and the front rooms were often rented out to businesses, including a barbershop, a tailor shop, and a fish market. It was also home to the department of education, the constable's office, and a jail. In 1913, additions were made to accommodate the Cheshire Fire Department and the Southern New England Telephone Company.

Photographer E.W. Hazard was on Southington Mountain on February 21, 1921. A runaway trolley had crashed, and he managed to tromp through the snow to record the mishap. It is said that the crash occurred in Cheshire, but no additional details are known.

E.W. Hazard was also on the scene of this truck crash in the Quinnipiac River in Cheshire. Apparently, the eight-ton truck was too heavy for the bridge and broke through, landing in the river. The sign on the side of the truck reads, "Storage Warehouse, Butterfield Street, Harrison."

Walter and Cora Abel of Waterbury liked to travel and commune with nature. Their daughter, Helen Abel, became a Cheshire resident as an adult. She married Burke Hoffman and lived on Waterbury Road in a former restaurant. This *c.* 1920 photograph shows her at age three with her parents and their dog upon their arrival at a campsite in the New England woods.

In this photograph, Helen and Cora Abel are standing by the tent, ready to rough it.

The Cheshire Fire Department poses for a portrait by photographer E.W. Hazard in September 1924. The fire trucks have been identified as Model T Fords of the 1920s. They were housed in the Cheshire Town Hall at the time. In the truck, on the left, are William Roberts and Everett Pardee. Seated are Edward Williams, Dexter Durand, Druire Bristol, George Keeler, Alfred Bennett, Willie French, John H.R. Bishop, Chief George Thorpe, Assistant Chief Allen

The Moss-Hyson home, located at 1067 Wolf Hill, was originally built in 1810 by Isaac Moss. At that time it was a simple, federal-style farmhouse. In 1860, Charles Ives and his family moved in and added an ell and a wraparound porch. William and Mary Peck resided here in the 1920s and 1930s. In 1950, Charles O. Dutton and his wife, Sophie, arrived and stayed until 1974. Sophie Dutton, now a widow, sold the home to Ernie and Betsy Strom, who remained for five years, modernized the house, dismantled the barn and carriage house, and added a swimming pool. Eric and Mary Hyson purchased the house in 1979 and raised their three children here. Mary Hyson is the sleuth who documented the history of the house.

Goddard, George Tucker, Paul Hotchkiss, Birdsey Norton, Edward Gillen, Robert Ives, Charles
Davis, Wesley Collins, and Tilton Munson. Standing are Robert Mattoon, Matt Haller, Leslie
Hubbell, Lester Hitchcock, Frank Peters, Oscar Gode, Raymond Hine, Lyle Terrel, Herman
Link, Frank Porter, Richard Williams, Robert Fen, Michael Sheehan, and Emerson Jeralds. In
the truck on the right are Emil Yocher and Charles Nelson.

Levi Peck (left) calms the horse for his friend on the lawn at 1067 Wolf Hill Road.

200TH ANNIVERSARY PAGEANT CHESHIRE CT SEPT 13TH 1924.

The 200th anniversary of the First Congregational Church was celebrated from September 12 to 14, 1924. One of the events was a series of tableaux tracing the history of the United States. Mrs. Frederick M. Peasley was the chairperson of the entire event. E.R. Brown, Mary Baldwin, Frederick A. Ives, and Jacob D. Walter were responsible for planning and staging the historical pageant. The event took place on the Roxbury Academy athletic fields, with musical accompaniment provided by the Cheshire Military Band. In the ensuing years, the photo postcards from the event became so rare that current residents, even experts on Cheshire history, could not identify the event. With some journalistic digging by Dave Kenny, Lillian Andrews, Martha Lape, and the author, the origin of the 22 sepia-toned postcards began to emerge from the archives of the church. Many of them—and there may be more—appear for the first time in this book. Although the photographer of the series is not identified, the pictures look like the work of E.W. Hazard and have title lettering that is very similar to that on his identified photographs. In this image, a Pilgrim protects a group of women and a young girl.

A Pilgrim leads a group in prayer.

Seen here are Pilgrims gathering and chopping wood. There are some deliberately scratched-out areas on this card and others in the series. The reason for this is unknown, although the photographer may have eliminated anachronisms in this way.

A Pilgrim leads a small group of women in prayer.

Pilgrim justice is administered at the whipping post.

Some Native Americans attend to their daily tasks.

This card is labeled on the back "Surprise Party." The scene is set in Colonial times.

Another scene set in Colonial times is labeled "Minuet" on the back of the card.

"Call to Arms" is the title of this scene set in the Revolutionary War era.

124

This card shows one of the most moving of the scenes, entitled "A Soldier's Farewell." A Civil War soldier says goodbye to two women, probably his wife and mother.

In the most dramatic of the tableaux, Pres. Abraham Lincoln frees a slave. A Confederate soldier turns his back on the symbolic event.

125

This emotional scene is entitled "When Johnny Comes Marching Home." If you listen carefully, you can almost hear the Cheshire Military Band performing the song in the background.

The steady trek of Father Time, hourglass in hand, is one constant we all share. Shown here is Howard "Pop" Durand, patriarch of the theatrical Durand family—Cheshire residents and famous vaudevillians. Alas, there is no more room for their story and images, but Sterling Jewett's book about them is available at the Cheshire Historical Society.

CONCLUSION

If you are able to shed any light on questions or mysteries raised by this book, or if my research and conclusions need redirecting, please contact me at home or through Arcadia Publishing. Thank you for your interest in the town of Cheshire and the book *Cheshire*.

I would like to thank all of the people who assisted me in the completion of this book, especially the entire staff of the Portsmouth, New Hampshire, office of Arcadia Publishing.

The following list is as complete as my 54-year-old memory will permit. I apologize if I have forgotten anyone. I once appeared on an author's acknowledgment page and it meant a lot to me; I would not want to deprive anyone of the experience.

I give many thanks to Eric Anderson, Lillian Andrews, Liz Acas, Pat Barbato, Dave Basconi, Ove Baskerud, Jo Byrolly, Judy Boynton, Ron Butler, Carol Ann Brown, Don Baillie, Margaret Boland, the Cheshire Historical Society, Tom Crowe, Katie Coleman, Fred Chesson, Ev Cassagneres, Ed Conklin, Elaine Conklin, Jeanne Chesanow, Clayton Crabtree, Rick Ciaburri, Bob Cawood, Paul Camerato, Dottie Drufva, Dr. Charles Dimmick, Duane Ellingson, Ralph and Jean Edson, Pam Guglielmino, Cliff Gilmond, Nancy and Tom Grenfell, Elizabeth Giardino, Ed Gumbrecht, Art Gumbus, Estelle Hayes, Burke Hoffman, Arthur Hostage, Claudette Hovasse, Mary Hobler Hyson, Maureen and Joe Jakubisyn, Allen Jones, Warren Jones, Sterling Jewett, Mike Johnson, Edgar Johnson, James Kwiatkowski, Dave Kenny, Ed Kania, August Loeb, Martha Lape, Aleta Looker, Betty, Pomp and Vinny Lentini, Jean Meek, Henry McNulty, Ann Moriarity, Dick Miller, James Meehan, John Martin, Lucille Norton, Joan Nardello, Walter Nuremburg, Ed O'Neill, William J. Pape II, Tim Pelton, Tom Pool, Mary Rossi, Jose Rodriguez, Ron Rising, Joe Raines, Cliff Scofield, Ed Spagnolo, Jerry Sitko, Ed Saad, Patricia Sepp, Laraine Smith, Southington Historical Society, Chris Tall, Dick Ulbrich, Inge Venus, Judge Ray Voelker, Pat Vita, John and Barbara White, Dora Whitright, Allen Wethers, and Ruth Yager.

ABOUT THE AUTHOR

Question: Who is this Ron Gagliardi person, and what gives him the audacity to presume he could compile and write this book on the town of Cheshire? Answer: Ron is a longtime resident of the town, who has lived in Cheshire since 1972. He and his wife, Diane, daughter, Gina, and son, Jeff, really enjoy living in Cheshire, having moved within town from Gateway Court to Buttonwood Circle to 5 Dover Court, their current residence.

Ron is vitally interested in Cheshire's past, present, and future. He is a life member of the Friends of the Library and the Cheshire Land Trust. He is also a life member of the Cheshire Historical Society and currently serves on the board of directors. He calls himself a "historyologist," one who connects the present with the past through research and commemorative ceremonies. His reenactment ceremony of John F. Kensett's memorial service for the 125th anniversary of his death on the site of his birth was well received in town. He also staged an event to commemorate the passage of the *Amistad* captives through Lock 12 on the Farmington Canal.

Ron has been an elementary art teacher for over 30 years and a professional videographer for over 20 years. He has written filmstrips, designed and captioned illustrations for a book, conceptualized and written animation scripts for a Public Television show, and penned seven years of weekly poems for the *Cheshire Herald* newspaper.

He also served two years on the Cheshire Town Council and was the public information officer for the Civil Defense Department in town. He chaired and helped found the Beautification Committee, was vice chair and chair of the Performing and Fine Arts Committee, vice chair of the Youth Services Committee, and vice chair of the Cable Advisory Committee. He has been a Cheshire Jaycee officer and a longtime member of the Cheshire Democratic Town Committee. He is a Justice of the Peace, and he was chosen as the town's first Mr. Cheshire in a spoof beauty pageant in 1975. Now, he hopes to be a Mr. Cheshire for a new reason, telling the story of the town's history to anyone who will listen.

www.ingramcontent.com/pod-product-compliance
Lightning Source LLC
Chambersburg PA
CBHW080853100426
42812CB00007B/2012